JAPANESE EXOTIC CARS

Photography by Henry Rasmussen
Text by Jack Doo

Motorbooks International
Publishers & Wholesalers Inc
Osceola, Wisconsin 54020, USA

First published in 1989 by Motorbooks International Publishers & Wholesalers Inc, P O Box 2, 729 Prospect Avenue, Osceola, WI 54020 USA

© Henry Rasmussen and Jack Doo, 1989

All rights reserved. With the exception of quoting brief passages for the purposes of review no part of this publication may be reproduced without prior written permission from the publisher

Motorbooks International is a certified trademark, registered with the United States Patent Office

Printed and bound in Hong Kong

The information in this book is true and complete to the best of our knowledge. All recommendations are made without any guarantee on the part of the author or publisher, who also disclaim any liability incurred in connection with the use of this data or specific details

We recognize that some words, model names and designations, for example, mentioned herein are the property of the trademark holder. We use them for identification purposes only. This is not an official publication.

Library of Congress
Cataloging-in-Publication Data
Rasmussen, Henry
   Japanese Exotic cars / photography by
  Henry Rasmussen ; text by Jack Doo.
    ISBN 0-87938-333-X
    1. Automobiles—Japan. 2. Automobiles—
  Japan—Pictorial works.
  I. Doo, Jack. II. Title.
TL105.R37 1989   88-29116
629.2'222'0952—dc19   CIP

Front cover: The daring lines of the old and the new, Japanese style: Nissan's Special Edition 300ZX Turbo alongside a classic Toyota 2000 GT. Back cover: A 1966 Honda S800 sports car faces off with Honda's latest Hurricane superbike. The S800 evolved from Honda's experience in building motorcycles. Frontispiece: With the Celica convertible dawns a new day for Toyota. Title page: A Yamaha-built Toyota 2000 GT at speed. Contents page: Toyota's "sweet sixteen" four-valve-per-cylinder powerplant made its debut in the 1986 Corolla GT-S. Introduction: The evolution of Japanese auto design, from the 1960s Datsun 2000 with its MGB-influenced lines to the Nissan 300ZX with lines all its own. Last page: A top view of the topless Toyota Celica.

Contents

Land of the rising sun   *6*

Era of imitation: 1930-59   *8*

Decade of innovation: 1960-69   *18*

The Japanese invasion: 1970-79   *50*

Decade of exotic technology: 1980 and on   *68*

Into the future   *116*

Land of the rising sun

Many of Japan's sports and grand touring cars are as exotic as *Kabuki*, the traditional Japanese theater.

As with its opera, Japan's automotive treasures combine intricate plots, lavish costumes, well-engineered drama and plenty of action.

While best known for its sea of utilitarian Toyotas, Nissans and Hondas that have made it the world's Number One automobile producer, another facet of Japanese cars is its exotics.

Japan's first exotic cars were exotic only for their historical significance for the time and culture. The first Japanese-made automobile in 1904 was a symbol that Japan was rejoining the world and the twentieth century.

This was a country that, just fifty years before, had shut itself off from the rest of the world for 250 years.

Since that humble beginning, marked by the Torao Yamaba-built motor vehicle, Japan has been a quick learner in the automotive world.

While its early efforts basically were copies of established American and European models, the ensuing decades brought such milestone cars as the Toyota 2000 GT, rotary-powered Mazda Cosmo and Datsun 240Z.

When it comes to the arena of exotic technology and innovation, the Japanese take a back seat to no one. As for the first production cars with exotic ceramic turbochargers, stratified charged engines, electronic active suspension or four-wheel steering? Look not to Ferrari, Porsche or Lamborghini, but to the land of the rising sun.

Era of imitation: 1930-59

An ancient Asian proverb states: "Before you can run, you must first learn to walk."

For the pioneer Japanese auto makers it could have been written: "Before you can innovate, you must first learn to imitate."

At the dawn of the Japanese auto industry, Japan was still a nation severely limited by the effect of an agricultural-based feudal system that had been in place for hundreds of years.

Japan was decades behind the industrial revolution being experienced by its European and American counterparts. While the early 1900s saw the auto industry thrive in Europe and the United States, a motor vehicle was but an oddity in Japan.

Automobiles were not much more than expensive playthings for Japan's rich. The few cars in Japan, mostly imported from the West, were considered toys. The acceptance and practicality of the automobile also was hampered by Japan's narrow and rough roads—easily traversed by the traditional man-powered rickshaws, but ill-suited for the so much larger automobile.

The virtues of the automobile were not to be denied, however, not even by the restrictive Japanese culture and environment.

In 1904, Torao Yamaba built the first Japanese-made motor vehicle. Yamaba, who created his steam-powered wagon to transport his large family, did not go beyond producing the original vehicle.

So the honor of manufacturing Japan's first true production car goes to Shintaro Yoshida and his Automobile Trading Company. Yoshida's firm, which had been assembling imported cars as early as 1902, introduced the Japanese-made Takuri in 1907. Dozens of the simple cars were built by the firm.

Designed by American-schooled Komanosuke Uchiyama, the Takuri borrowed heavily from various European cars, including the Darracq and Laurin & Klement.

The Takuri Type 3 was powered by a twin-cylinder, horizontally-opposed engine displacing 1850 cc. The two-speed transmission channeled the engine's 12 hp to the rear wheels via twin chain drives. Semi-elliptic springs at each corner suspended the four wheels from the steel, box-type ladder frame. The wood-framed steel body featured a pair of bench seats for passengers.

The Takuri established the copycat philosophy most Japanese auto makers would practice out of necessity for decades to follow. Imitation, not innovation, would be the fastest way for Japan to close its automotive technical gap with Europe and the United States.

Some of the most notable Japanese clones during the early automotive years were produced by Datsun and Toyota.

The first car to carry the Datsun name was the Type 10 in 1931. The Type 10, inspired by the 1922 Austin Seven, had a 495 cc four-cylinder powerplant with side valves. The following year the displacement was enlarged to 744 cc. The first Datsuns were popular as taxis. Later versions in 1935-37 were available as a sedan, or in a smart roadster version.

Other Japanese clones were produced through technical agreements or under license with various auto makers. The Nissan—Datsun's parent company's name—Type 70 bowed in 1936, the result of a technical union between Nissan and Graham-Paige in America. The Type 70 was a larger, six-cylinder car offered as a sedan or phaeton.

A similar licensing agreement saw Isuzu producing and marketing vehicles designed by the English firm Wolseley. Other collaborations teamed Mitsubishi with Kaiser Motor Company, Isuzu with Rootes and Hino with Renault.

When Kiichiro Toyoda, heir to a successful modern textile machine business, decided to go into automobile manufacturing, he chose to copy the best.

His first Toyota Motor Company prototype was the 1935 A-1, a look-alike for the Chrysler Airflow, one of the most advanced American automobiles for the period.

Toyoda later looked to Swedish auto maker Volvo for inspiration for the 1943 BA model, which would resemble the Volvo PV60.

Toyoda covered new ground with the 1955 Toyota Crown, recognized as the first authentic all-Japanese car. However, that distinction helped to make exports of the Crown to the United States a flop in 1957. This truly Japanese car was not equipped to handle the long distances and relatively high speeds found in the United States—just the opposite of Japanese driving conditions of the time.

Another purely Japanese innovation was the Midget car concept. The micro-minis came about as the result of a taxation system based on engine displacement. The less than 360 cc category was taxed much less than the two larger divisions. The Midgets also were more affordable, could share engine technology with the more established motorcycle industry and were better suited to the Japanese roads of the time.

The egg-shaped Subaru 360 appeared in 1958 and was typical of the Midget car class. Other early Midget competitors included the Suzuki Suzulight, Mazda R-360 and Mitsubishi Minica.

This beautifully restored 1937 Datsun Roadster, shown here and on the preceding page, is owned by Nissan Motor Corporation U.S.A. It is the final variation of the first Datsun-labeled car that was introduced in 1932. The Datsun name goes back to 1911 when three Japanese entrepreneurs named Den, Aoyama and Takeuchi built a crude, but workable car. They combined their first initials and called it DAT, which means "fast rabbit" in Japanese. A new car in 1931 was named Datson, or son of DAT. Soon the name was changed to Datsun in deference to the ancient Japanese sun symbol. As with most of the early models produced by Japanese auto makers, the two-passenger Datsun roadster was a copy of an established marque. Though the car had an electric starter, the Datsun roadster came equipped with a backup crank starter. Interestingly, all Datsuns produced through 1966 had provisions for a crank starter. The later models of the Datsun roadster, in sedan and convertible variations, also had a longer wheelbase. The roadster boasted a trunk that opened into a rumble seat for additional passengers. Production of the first Datsun peaked at 15,000 units in 1937.

Looking for a heavenly sign is Subaru 360 owner Louis Crank. Crank's worldly attentions are focused on his micro-mini car, a rare Maia convertible. The perky 360 was introduced in 1958, and brought the midget car era and affordable driving to Japanese consumers. The egg-shaped 360 was designed by the same technical staff that created the famed Mitsubishi Zero World War II fighter plane. The Zero designers engineered the economy car to have state-of-the-art features such as a rear-mounted, two-stroke, air-cooled engine layout, synchronized transmission and four-wheel independent torsion bar suspension. The advanced design, which was also available as a station wagon, allowed the Subaru 360 to be produced through 1971. Entrepreneur Malcolm Bricklin imported the 360 into the United States and while sales of the little car did not exactly take off, Bricklin later regrouped and established what is now Subaru of America. Crank, a Las Vegas, Nevada, resident, keeps his out-of-production 360 in peak running condition, with assistance from the national Subaru 360 Drivers' Club. The active group is based in Tucson, Arizona, and has nearly 600 of the diminutive runabouts in its membership.

Surprisingly, the Subaru 360, while small on the outside, is relatively large inside. The enterprising Subaru designers were able to squeeze four individual seats between the 360's 71 inch wheelbase and 117¾ inch length. The space-saving seats are simply foam rubber cushions over ribbed steel pressings. The rear seatbacks hinge forward to increase luggage capacity, an innovative feature commonly used in contemporary cars. The driving controls were kept simple—one instrument gauge and switches for the starter and choke—because at the car's introduction, driving was a new experience in Japan. Motivation for the 360 came from a two-stroke, two-cylinder powerplant displacing 356 cc and producing 16 hp at 4500 rpm. The performance Maia version had a 422 cc engine that pushed horsepower to 22. A three-speed synchronized transmission was upgraded to four speeds in 1969. Standard 360 models had a top speed of 52 mph and sipped the gas-oil fuel mix at the rate of 73 mpg.

Two major design features that maximize interior space efficiency in the Subaru 360 are the rear-mounted powerplant and the wheels. The alloy engine and transaxle package is hung outside of the passenger compartment. The louvered vents above the rear-wheel arches are an air supply source to the air-cooled engine. The wide-opening hinged hood provides excellent access to the powerplant for service and maintenance work. Ten-inch steel wheels are mounted on matching 4.50 size tires. The small tires intrude little into the passenger area and are key to the car's extremely small turning circle. For having such small tires, the 360 is noted for its excellent ride and handling. Credit goes to the progressive suspension that features independently sprung torsion bars at each corner. Subaru also engineered-in a large range of wheel travel to cope with the potholes, raised tram rails and the generally hostile conditions that marked Japanese roadways of the time.

Decade of innovation: 1960-69

Car fever hit Japan in the 1960s and Japanese auto makers were ready with the cure. The prescription was not limited to econoboxes, but included milestone sports and racing models.

The healthy growth of Japan's economy energized the building industry, which created a demand for trucks and forced the development of roads. Industrialization also spawned the growth of suburbs to house workers. Workers needed mobility to get to work, and that meant the automobile.

The industrialization of Japan brought the price of the car down and increased income per capita, thus making the automobile very affordable.

With practical economy cars well established, the Japanese turned to sports and grand touring models. For Japanese auto engineers it was no longer mandatory to design for Japan's ninety-nine-percentile motorists. They were freed to create some new, exciting and exotic designs. Paralleling this development was increased involvement in auto racing.

Datsun introduced its line of Fairlady sports cars in 1959. The S211 Sport was the first of the series of open sports cars for the auto maker. The initial model was followed by a more powerful SP213 with 60 hp.

Next came the popular Datsun 1600 and 2000 roadsters, obviously influenced by traditional British sports cars made by Triumph, MG and Austin-Healey. A successful Sports Car Club of America racing program and the resulting National Championships, helped to establish Datsun as a legitimate sports car manufacturer to American auto enthusiasts.

The success of the small roadsters paved the way for Datsun's 240Z coupe. The Z series, which would become the most popular Japanese sports car ever, was conceived after Datsun engineers had studied nearly every sports car design in the world. In the 240Z, influenced by noted German designer Albert Goertz, can be seen glimpses of Jaguar's E Type and various Ferrari models.

Honda first ventured into the auto world in 1962 with the S500 sports car. The motorcycle giant integrated much of its vast two-wheel expertise into the S500 roadster, making it a true auto exotic of the time.

The S500 boasted a four-cylinder powerplant that pumped out 44 hp at 8000 rpm—amazingly high rpm for an automobile. The jewel-like engine had twin overhead camshafts and four sidedraft carburetors.

Toyota answered the Honda sports car challenge with its Sports 800. And then, Toyota got serious about the sports car market with the release of its world-class 2000 GT in 1965.

An equally exotic Japanese model was the Mazda Cosmo 110S that was unveiled at the Tokyo Motor Show of 1964. Though radically styled, a near copy of the Ferrari Super America, the most exotic component of the Cosmo was its twin-rotor Wankel engine.

The spirit of the rotary-powered Cosmo lived on with the RX-2 rotary sedan that established Mazda in the United States in the 1970s, and the acclaimed RX-7 sports car that came in 1978.

Japanese auto makers used racing in the sixties to refine, improve and promote their products.

As with passenger cars, the Japanese once again found themselves behind and trying to catch up in racing. It was not until the 1963 Japanese Grand Prix that Japan was recognized as a serious competitor in modern auto racing.

Nissan, Toyota, Mazda and Isuzu had varying successes at the annual Japanese Grand Prix showdown with its European counterparts, but it was in the premier Grand Prix Formula One circuit that Honda proved that Japanese innovation and technology were world class.

The ambitious Honda Formula One program began in 1962, with the first Honda open-wheel racer turning a wheel in 1964. Once again drawing from its motorcycle experience and numerous two-wheel world titles, the heart of the Honda effort was its 1.5 liter, V-12 powerplant.

Taking on Grand Prix powerhouses such as Ferrari, Brabham and Lotus, American Ritchie Ginther scored Honda's first Formula One victory at Mexico City in October 1965. Honda's second win, the first in the new three-liter formula, came at Monza, Italy, in 1967 with former world champion John Surtees at the wheel.

Honda subsequently withdrew from Formula One after the following season, but returned to the premier racing series in 1983. Honda's 1.5 liter, turbocharged V-6 engine ultimately powered the Williams team and driver Nelson Piquet to the World Championship in 1986.

Honda power in 1988 was used by the Lotus and McLaren teams, with McLaren teammates Ayrton Senna and Alain Prost dominating the Grand Prix circuit.

The Datsun 1600 was the Japanese version of the traditional English sports car. Like its Austin-Healey, MG and Triumph rivals, the 1600 was straightforward in layout—a front-mounted engine driving the rear wheels. In addition to better reliability and a heater that actually worked, the 1600's main advantage over its British counterparts was in its excellent value. The long list of standard equipment included full synchromesh four-speed transmission, front disc brakes, radio, roll-up windows, electric clock, tachometer, tonneau cover, trip meter, full carpeting and seatbelts. All this could be had for just $2,546 in 1967. The only better bargain was the Datsun 2000, which added a 135 hp, two-liter engine and five-speed gearbox to the 1600 formula for only $330 over the 1600. In addition, a Solex-carburetor version of the 2000 powerplant also was available and rated at 150 hp. During the production years 1966-71, Datsun took to the racetracks to prove the 1600 and 2000 in competition. The cars did not disappoint, with the 1600 grabbing the Sports Car Club of America F Production National title and the 2000 staking claim to the D Production division.

The most popular early Japanese sports car imported to the United States was the Datsun 1600. Introduced in 1962 in Japan, the roadster was loosely based on the traditional British sports car. The half-buried headlight design is straight from the MGB. The 1600 was powered by a 1.6 liter, four-cylinder engine rated at 96 hp at 6000 rpm. According to factory figures, the 1600 could sprint 0-60 mph in 11 seconds and had a top speed of 106 mph. The engine of the 1600 also was a close clone to the British offerings. Under the hood, the powerplant looks much like an MG unit from the placement of the distributor to the sidedraft carburetor. The two 38 mm carburetors look exactly like the SU carburetor used on the MG, but actually are Japanese Hitachi units manufactured under a licensing agreement with SU. This pristine 1970 1600 is owned by the Nissan Motor Corporation USA and is part of the firm's ten-car collection of "milestone" cars.

Honda's latest Hurricane superbike and its vintage S800 sports car counterpart share a common heritage. Each was spawned from Honda's vast experience from building motorcycles since 1949. Honda used its knowledge as the world's largest motorcycle manufacturer to create its first car, the S500 sports car. The S500 had a 78.7 inch wheelbase, an overall length of 131.3 inches and tipped the scales at 1,556 pounds. In the small Honda's engine and drivetrain can be found its two-wheel heritage. The four-cylinder, 531 cc powerplant peaked at 44 hp at a motorcycle-like 8000 rpm. The power was transmitted through chain drives, a separate chain for each rear axle. The S500 had a top speed of 85 mph. The S500 in 1963 evolved into the S600 with a larger 606 cc engine rated at 57 hp and topping out at 90 mph. The S600 was available as a roadster or coupe. The ultimate S series Honda was the S800 which was built from 1966 through 1969, shown also on the chapter's opening pages.

The powerplant in the Honda S800 sports car would look at home under the hood of the roadster or between the legs of a motorcyclist. A brace of four sidedraft Keihin carburetors add to the motorcycle look. The S800 engine displaces 791 cc and is rated at 70 hp. Other motorcycle technology found in the S800 engine includes double overhead cams, hemispherical cylinder heads and an 8000 rpm redline. Honda today mounts engines larger than the S800's into its superbikes. The CBR1000F Hurricane two-wheeler displaces 998 cc and has an amazing 130 hp. However, on a long journey and definitely in foul weather, the S800's comfortable interior and weatherproof folding soft top would win out over the potent motorcycle. The snug cockpit, outfitted with full instrumentation, supportive bucket seats, four-speed transmission and wood-trimmed steering wheel makes good use of the car's narrow 55.1 inch width. The S sports cars from Honda were limited-production models and are considered rare and collectible.

While the Mazda Cosmo 110S had exotic lines borrowed from the Ferrari Super America, its truly exotic components were under the hood. The Wankel-powered sports car was unveiled at the Tokyo Motor Show of 1964 and reached showroom floors by 1967. Mazda, the only automobile manufacturer to develop and continue to produce rotary-powered cars, acquired a license from NSU to build the unique powerplant. The original Cosmo coupe had a 982 cc, twin-rotor engine rated at 111 hp and was the first Wankel engine to be mass produced. While the Cosmo was a limited-production sports car that ended its production run in 1972, it established the viability of the rotary engine. By 1973, Mazda had sold 500,000 vehicles with the revolutionary powerplant and surpassed the million mark just five years later. Mazda continues today as the world's sole producer of rotary-powered vehicles. In the spirit of the Cosmo, Mazda's most successful rotary car ever is another sports car, the acclaimed RX-7.

Mazda's first Wankel-powered car had to be special, so the Japanese clothed the unique powerplant with a sleek exterior that is close to the Ferrari Super America. Making for interesting proportions was the long overhang behind the rear wheels. Clues that the Cosmo 110S was for Japanese consumption only are the covered headlights, mid-fender-mounted sideview mirrors and right-hand drive. For a Japanese car of the period, the Cosmo was extremely understated with a minimum of chrome and identification badges. While not a Ferrari V-12, the Cosmo 110S powerplant was even more exotic at the time. Produced under a license from Wankel, the Mazda proved with the Cosmo that the rotary engine had a future; Wankel engines became a regular feature on Mazda vehicles both in production and on the racetrack.

The Mazda Cosmo 110S instrumentation included a mandatory tachometer in front of the driver. This was a must as the rotary engine is so smooth and quiet; the rev counter is the only indication the engine is running. The rotary engine uses a third of the number of parts compared to a piston powerplant and is simple in design and layout. Note the twin distributors and the two spark plugs for each rotor. The initial 110S prototype had a twin-rotor engine rated at 70 hp. By the car's debut in 1967, horsepower of the 982 cc twin-rotor engine had jumped to 111. In the next five years, Mazda engineers had pushed the horsepower to 128. As of 1988, a turbocharged rotary RX-7 is rated at 182 hp. Mazda also has prototype RX-7s running around with normally aspirated three-rotor engines pumping out 220 hp.

Toyota tread new ground in creating its Sports 800 sports car in 1965. Unlike rival Nissan, Toyota did not opt to merely clone traditional British sports cars. Toyota's version of two-seat motoring fun was like no other sportster past or present. It also was smaller than most other sports cars with a wheelbase of 78.7 inches and an overall length of just 142.1 inches. The car's 28 foot turning circle made it perfect for navigating Japan's narrow streets. A featherweight at 1,280 pounds, the Sports 800's trim weight was enhanced by a unique, twin-cylinder, air-cooled powerplant. The 790 cc engine, mated to a four-speed synchromesh transmission, pushed the Toyota sports car to a top speed of 97 mph. In fuel economy, the Sports 800 was in motorcycle territory with a factory figure of 57.9 mpg. An eight-gallon fuel tank gave a driving range of more than 450 miles. The independent front suspension uses torsion bars and is matched with a solid rear axle suspended by semi-elliptic leaf springs. The unit-body Sports 800 rolls on 12 inch wheels and 6.00 tires. Toyota never exported the limited-production car—a loss for the rest of the motoring world.

The powerplant of the Toyota Sports 800 shares many traits with the sports car it's mounted in—it is unique, lightweight and innovative. The two-cylinder engine is air cooled and has a pair of horizontally opposed cylinders. The closest comparison to the 790 cc overhead valve engine would be to the four in a 1965 Porsche 912. However, the Toyota goes beyond Stuttgart engineering with features such as hydraulic lifters and hemispherical cylinder heads. The engine breathes through twin downdraft single-barrel carburetors that pump up the output of the diminutive powerplant to 49 hp at 5400 rpm. The alloy engine with clutch weighs just 176 pounds. The Sports 800 again can be compared to the Porsche, each with a removable Targa top for open-air motoring. The interior of the Toyota two-seater is basic sports car with four major instruments directly in front of the driver and a sporting three-spoke steering wheel. This particular example is a rare left-hand-drive model.

The Toyota 2000 GT is a world-class exotic car. Produced in extremely limited production from 1965 to 1968, the 2000 GT had it all—style, flare, performance, a racing history linked with Carroll Shelby and even a starring role in a James Bond 007 movie. The lines of the 2000 GT are reminiscent of the Jaguar XKE. The Yamaha-built powerplant also was very XKE-like—an inline six displacing two-liters and producing 150 hp. The 2000 GT was good for 130 mph and if that was not enough, a competition version churned out 200 hp. That's where Cobra creator Shelby comes in. Toyota contracted with Shelby to campaign a pair of 2000 GTs in the Sports Car Club of America's C Production category. With Porsche ace Scooter Patrick at the wheel, the car was competitive in the hotly contested National series. Toyota soon canceled production of its GT cars and the project was concluded, however. In addition to the racetrack, the 2000 GT also starred in the movies. A pair of 2000 GT coupes had their tops removed—the two cars are the only convertible 2000 GTs ever made—for the 1967 James Bond movie *You Only Live Twice*, which was filmed on location in Japan.

Yamaha incorporated many of its advanced motorcycle innovations when it designed the powerplant for the Toyota 2000 GT. The beautifully detailed engine displaces 1988 cc and breathes through three two-barrel, sidedraft Mikuni-Solex 40 PHH carburetors. The double overhead cam engine produces 150 hp at 6600 rpm and has a 7000 rpm redline. The compression ratio is 8.4:1 and torque is rated at 130 lb-ft at a peaky 5000 rpm. A more powerful competition version used racing tweaks like a higher compression ratio and more radical cams to gain 50 hp over the base unit. The jewel-like engine is mated to a five-speed manual gearbox. The close-ratio transmission and 4.375:1 final drive emphasizes acceleration and limits the top speed of the 2000 GT to about 130 mph. Yamaha mounted the engine in a steel backbone frame with a welded, semi-unit body. Suspension was independent at all four corners with unequal-length A-arms, coil springs and front and rear antiroll bars. Yamaha continues its research and development relationship with Toyota. Most recently Yamaha designed and developed the production Toyota MR2 and MR2 Supercharged 1.6 liter engines.

The interior of the Toyota 2000 GT is very straightforward and ergonomically functional, with 160 mph speedometer and 9000 rpm tachometer located directly in front of the driver. The layout featured a full complement of instruments including a rally clock and signal-seeking AM radio with electric antenna. Other interior highlights included a heated rear window and the inlaid wood dash. The bucket seats reclined and the interior had good space utilization for the 164.4 inch length. The setback position of the passenger compartment and fastback styling helped the 2000 GT achieve a weight distribution of 48 percent front and 52 percent back. The weight balance contributed to the car's excellent handling and performance from the four-wheel disc brakes. The small production run of the 2000 GT did not justify tying up any of Toyota's production capacity, so the manufacturing of the 2,480 pound coupe was farmed out to Yamaha. The motorcycle maker produced only 337 of the state-of-the-art GTs, with just 53 finding their way to the United States. Though it has not since built complete cars, Yamaha continues its association with Toyota and has participated in more than two dozen engine programs.

The Japanese invasion: 1970-79

Exotic technology and performance models took the Japanese auto center stage in the 1970s. Leading the way were sophisticated powerplants that utilized such features as stratified charged ignition, lean-burning twin spark plug cylinder heads, balance shafts and external-combustion rotary engines.

The emphasis on high tech was spurred by the search for more fuel efficiency and reduced emissions. Honda and Datsun both found the solution in super-lean air-fuel mixtures, but took different paths to achieve the same results.

The engineers at Honda came up with the first production stratified charge engine it called CVCC, for Compound Vortex Controlled Combustion. Introduced on the 1972 Civic, the design featured an auxiliary combustion chamber where the spark plug and an additional intake valve were located. The extra chamber ignited a rich fuel mixture that then ignited the lean mixture of the main combustion chamber.

Datsun's NAP-Z (Nissan Anti-Pollution System Z) utilized a special-shaped combustion chamber and two spark plugs for each cylinder to light lean fuel mixtures.

To smooth out the inherent vibrations of its three-cylinder Charade, Daihatsu developed counter-rotating balance shafts to counteract the imbalance. Mitsubishi followed with its own balance shaft design, one so effective that Porsche licenses it for use in its 944 sports car.

The list of auto makers that invested millions of dollars in the Wankel engine and then gave up on the external-combustion powerplant includes NSU, Mercedes-Benz, Citroen and General Motors.

However, Mazda, which acquired a license from NSU in 1961, did not give up on the rotary engine. The Japanese auto maker had its first rotary model in showrooms in 1967 and continued to refine the unit.

Mazda's limited-production rotary-powered Cosmo sports car was produced from 1964 through 1972. The rotary came to the United States in the 1971 Mazda RX-2. Sales of the excellent-performing RX-2 sports sedan were extremely strong, until federal fuel-economy tests revealed the engine to be powerful, but thirsty. With sales taking a nose dive, Mazda pulled its rotary offerings from showrooms and began pushing its conventional, piston-engined GLC economy car.

Meanwhile, Mazda engineers continued to develop the rotary engine, waiting for another chance and knowing if it was not accepted this time around, it would probably spell the end of the Wankel.

The right development, the right time and the right car came together in the spring of 1978, when the 1979 Mazda RX-7 sports car was introduced and was an instant hit. The smooth and powerful engine was perfect for a sports car. The much improved fuel economy also was a less critical buying factor for sports car fans.

The RX-7 was aimed at the affordable sports car market that Datsun had successfully developed a niche in with its 240Z sports car. When introduced in the United States in 1970, the two-seater Datsun sold for less than $4,000 and had a huge following.

Datsun used racing to promote the 240Z and its 510 sports sedan in the US market. Brock Racing Enterprises (BRE), represented the West Coast and Bob Sharp took care of the competition on the East Coast. The quick and good-handling 510 sedan and driver John Morton won the Sports Car Club of America Trans-Am series in 1971 and 1972, defeating the more expensive entries from Alfa Romeo and BMW.

Datsun published a "how-to" book on modifying and hot-rodding its Z-car and 510 models. The publication included a catalog of trick factory parts available from local dealerships. Aftermarket firms such as BRE and Motorsport Industries soon followed with their own line of suspension kits, engine parts and fiberglass air dams, spoilers and flared fenders.

Toyota got into auto racing in 1977 by sponsoring a Pro/Celebrity race as part of the Grand Prix Formula One weekend at Long Beach, California. In 1980, Toyota became the major sponsor of the Grand Prix race through the streets and the annual event was renamed the Toyota Grand Prix of Long Beach.

The Toyota Pro/Celebrity race pits a field of about 20 professional and celebrity drivers against each other in a ten-lap race around the Formula One course in identically prepared Celica GTs. To even out the competition, the celebrities are given a head start.

Celebrities who have participated include Dick Smothers, Gene Hackman, Paul Williams, Clint Eastwood and Bruce Jenner. The Pros have been represented by Sam Posey, Willy T. Ribbs, Dan Gurney, Rick Mears, David Hobbs and Al Unser.

The Pro/Celebrity event, with a generous purse divided among the drivers' favorite charities, continues as a real crowd pleaser and a perfect promotion for Toyota—a Toyota is guaranteed to win.

Nissan did its homework in studying every successful sports and grand touring car before designing the Datsun 240Z. The Z-car has a bit of Ferrari and Jaguar XKE in its exterior, as shown on the preceding pages. The car became an instant success when introduced in the United States in 1970 with a base sticker price of $3,526. Buyers were willing to place deposits and stand in line to buy the 240Z. The new car offered a refined six-cylinder engine displacing 2.4 liters and producing 150 hp at 6000 rpm. Carburetion was by a pair of sidedraft Hitachis. The potent engine was mated to a four-speed transmission. The chassis was as refined as the powerplant, with four-wheel independent suspension and front disc brakes. The two-seat fastback had a wide-opening rear hatch for easy access to the generous luggage compartment. With a wheelbase of 90.7 inches and an overall length of 162.8 inches, the 240Z weighed in at 2,355 pounds.

The 1970 Datsun 240Z was a milestone car for the Japanese auto industry—the first Japanese sports car to sell in numbers in the United States and worldwide. The 240Z created and developed the mid-range GT concept of blending sports car acceleration and handling with more emphasis on comfort and luxury. The heart of the 240Z is its smooth-running, overhead cam engine. The basic engine has stood the test of time and kept pace with the competition with displacement increases to 2.6 liters and then finally 2.8 liters. From its life from 1970 to the 1983 280ZX, the venerable six had been refined with the latest in fuel injection and ultimately turbocharging. The inline six was finally replaced in 1984 with the debut of the V-6 300ZX. Overall, the Z-car has been a huge success for Nissan. Since 1970 Nissan has sold more than 750,000 of its Z-cars. And it all started with the 240Z.

The success of the Datsun Z-car series also spawned a huge following of aftermarket firms ready with parts and accessories to personalize the sleek two-seater. Motorsport Industries, BRE, Impact Parts, Bob Sharp Racing, Far Performance and Dobi are among the past and present firms catering to the Z-car. The range of modifications runs from mild to wild, for show or for go. In the performance department, there are suspension kits with larger antiroll bars, firmer shock absorbers and shorter and stiffer coil springs. There are dozens of alloy wheel and performance tire combinations, including the popular Plus 1 and 2 concept for up to 17 inch tires. In the engine compartment, the long list of aftermarket parts includes a trio of sidedraft Weber carburetors, turbochargers and even a kit to bolt-in a small-block Chevrolet V-8 engine. On the cosmetic side, this Motorsport Industries–enhanced 280Z is a good example. The dress-up kit includes aero side skirts, front and rear spoilers and a clean rear valance-bumper combination.

If ever there was such a thing as a Giant Killer, that title would have to go to the Datsun 510. The overambitious economy car from Japan took on Alfa Romeo and BMW in contesting the Sports Car Club of America Trans-Am series' Under 2.5 Liter division. To help even the odds, Datsun enlisted the help of Pete Brock, Trevor Harris and John Morton. Brock, formerly with the Carroll Shelby Cobra racing team, handled the team manager duties; Harris took care of the chassis setup, and Morton did the driving. The vintage 510 sedan still lives in SCCA competition, and is a popular and winning car in the Improved Touring C division. Many of the 510 racers sport the classic BRE red-white-and-blue color scheme.

The RX-7 offered sleek lines, excellent handling and the smooth power of the Wankel rotary engine, all for a base sticker price of less than $7,000. It was in the RX-7 that the Wankel engine finally found a home. Earlier, after initial success, Mazda was forced to withdraw its rotary sedans from the US market when a poor showing in the federal fuel-economy ratings created a slump in sales. Mazda engineers knew that when they brought the rotary back to the United States it had to be right—in performance and fuel economy—or the Wankel would be dead forever. In the RX-7, the Wankel was right. The performance was right, with excellent driveability and 0-60 mph times under nine seconds. In overall fuel economy, the RX-7 easily averaged 20 mpg and nearly 30 on the highway. At the racetracks, the RX-7 proved nothing short of amazing. After placing first and second in their debut at the 1979 24 Hours of Daytona, RX-7 teams have gone on to win the IMSA GTU class for under-three-liter sports cars eight straight times.

Mazda engineers were smart to surround its innovative rotary engine with a simple design. The RX-7 has a conventional front-engine, rear-wheel-drive layout with a well-controlled solid rear axle. The 95.3 inch wheelbase and 170 inch overall length carries 2,128 pounds. The car rides on 13 inch wheels and 185/70-13 radial tires. The body design features a sloping hood with concealed headlights that flip up. The functional body is highlighted and accented by a black bumper strip that surrounds and protects the car's midline. The package is finished off with a clever rear hatch made entirely of glass. The well-appointed interior features supportive bucket seats and full instrumentation. Two trim levels were offered, the base S and the GS, which added alloy wheels and a five-speed gearbox. In 1981, a GSL luxury model was added that featured leather seats, power windows, cruise control, four-wheel disc brakes and a limited-slip differential. The RX-7 proved once again that the best ideas are the simplest.

The Toyota Celica was the Japanese auto maker's first entry in the fast-growing pony car field. Introduced in the home market in 1970, the Celica made it to US shores the following year and began establishing Toyota as a maker of more than just economy cars. The sporty Celica styling emphasized the long hood, short deck made popular by the Ford Mustang. The Celica was aimed at challenging the Mustang and other US pony cars. The Celica first appeared as a coupe and later was offered as a liftback, again following the Mustang that was available in coupe and fastback versions. Built on a 95.5 inch wheelbase with an overall length of 168.2 inches, the Celica tipped the scales at 2,300 pounds. Powering the Toyota sports coupe was a four-cylinder engine displacing two liters and producing 97 hp at 5500 rpm. A four-speed manual transmission was standard with an automatic optional. Later versions added fuel injection to the Celica engine which ultimately grew to 2.4 liters.

Following the success of Toyota Celica notchback coupe was a GT Liftback version in 1974. Notice that the fastback design and six taillights are very similar to the Ford Mustang's of the era. The next generation of Celicas reached US shores in 1978, followed by the third generation in 1983 and the fourth in 1986. In a unique shot, the second-and fourth-generation cars—in Toyota Grand Prix of Long Beach Pro/Celebrity race trim—can be compared nose-to-tail. The cars are the ones used by American racing great and Toyota spokesperson Dan Gurney during the annual charity race in Long Beach, California. Gurney also is the team manager for the Toyota Celica race team that won the 1987 IMSA GTO manufacturer's championship with drivers Chris Cord, Dennis Aase and Willy T. Ribbs. Cord, grandson of the founder of the Cord automobile, claimed the driver's title.

Decade of exotic technology: 1980 and on

Japan in the 1980s took leadership in sports and grand touring cars. Many of the Japanese sporting offerings are truly exotic in design with such innovations as mid-engines, concept car styling, multi-valve powerplants, superchargers, turbocharged rotaries and high-performance all-wheel drives.

The most exotic production car of today? That honor probably goes to the $200,000 Porsche 959. The German supercar has electronically-controlled four-wheel drive and a turbocharged engine. For about one tenth the price, Japan offers the next closest thing to a 959.

Both the Subaru XT6 and the Toyota Celica All-Trac have many of the 959 attributes. The XT6, like the Porsche, is powered by a flat-six engine and has electronic four-wheel drive and ride height control.

The Celica All-Trac teams its four-wheel-drive layout with a potent 190 hp powerplant that is turbocharged and intercooled like the 959. Both the All-Trac and the 959 use an antilock brake system.

Toyota in the 1980s also has been mounting sophisticated four-valve cylinder heads on everything from the entry-level Corolla to the flagship Supra personal luxury tourer. And Toyota goes one step further with the MR2 Supercharged.

The success of the MR2 and Honda's nifty CRX in the affordable sports car market were two reasons for the demise of Pontiac's mid-engine Fiero. Pontiac ended production of the plastic-bodied Fiero in the fall of 1988.

Japan's efficiency allows it to get a new-car design into production faster than any other car-building nation.

According to Robert Templin, a former chief engineer of General Motors' Cadillac Division and now a private consultant, Toyota has developed a system that could allow it to restyle its cars annually.

Isuzu displayed equally quick progress by taking a car from the concept stage to a production car in two years. In 1979, Isuzu needed a showstopper to prove to the automotive world it was a contender. It turned to noted Italian designer Giorgio Giugiaro to lend some credibility. Giugiaro came up with an exotic, radically sleek, wedge-shaped car called the Ace of Clubs.

The most exotic and hottest innovation in the 1980s is four-wheel steering. The first two production cars with this technical wizardry were from Japan. The Honda Prelude Si 4WS and Mazda GT in 1988 were the first to offer this handling breakthrough.

Four-wheel steering turns the rear wheels counter to the front at low speeds to enhance maneuvers such as parking. At higher speeds the rear tires are turned in the same direction as the fronts to greatly improve tracking and cornering ability.

The latest exotic Japanese entries are moving upscale. Honda was first to launch its "premium" Acura line and sold more than 50,000 Legend sedans and Integra sports sedans in its 1986 debut. Acura added the Legend Coupe the following year. The Coupe was a match of the BMW 6 Series for tens of thousands less.

Toyota and Nissan jumped on the bandwagon and immediately announced their own premium lines. Toyota's Lexus and Nissan's Infiniti made their debuts in the fall of 1989 and feature thirty-two-valve, V-8 powerplants.

Japan's exotic and sports cars are the image makers and flagships of what has become the Number One auto-producing nation. The Japanese auto industry, in its infancy in the 1960s, amazingly took over world leadership by the 1980s. The Japanese have set the world standard in design, quality, technology and manufacturing.

Japanese imports account for twenty-five percent of all new autos sold in the United States and fifty percent of the sales in trend-setting California. In addition to cars, America is importing Japanese manufacturing methods through partnerships and joint ventures based in the United States.

Japanese auto makers and their US partners include Toyota and General Motors in Fremont, California; Mazda and Ford Motor Company in Flat Rock, Michigan; and Mitsubishi and Chrysler Corporation in Normal, Illinois.

With Honda, Toyota, Isuzu, Subaru and Nissan having US plants, it is estimated that by 1990 a third of all passenger vehicles produced in the United States will have a Japanese heritage.

Honda, in 1984, created the ultimate expression of its Civic economy-car line, the CRX sports car. Built on the same basic platform as the utilitarian Civic sedans and wagons, the CRX made use of a compact fastback design over the 86.6 inch wheelbase. The CRX, which came to the United States in 1985, lived up to Honda's slogan of Economy Fast. The CRX HF used a 1.3 liter engine with a low-friction design to achieve 52 mpg in the US federal economy tests. The standard CRX model used a 1.5 liter engine. The high-performance CRX Si was added in 1986 with a fuel-injected engine rated at 91 hp. That may not sound like much, but when there is only 1,978 pounds to motivate, it translates to 0-60 mph in less than nine seconds. The CRX has been a tough competitor at racetracks. In addition to victories in Sports Car Club of America's Showroom Stock division, a CRX won the International Ice Racing Association title with P. D. Cunningham at the wheel.

Improving on a good thing, Honda in 1988 rolled out the next generation of its CRX sports car. This popular Japanese sportster was bigger and better than the previous model. While maintaining the same family resemblance and 147.8 inch length, Honda extended the wheelbase four inches to 90.6 inches, and widened the front and rear track two inches. The result was more interior space and a much improved ride. In all its stretching of the CRX, Honda was able to lower the car an inch and improve its coefficient of drag to just 0.30, a good trick with such a short car. A new functional styling feature was the rear of the deck lid that had a clear glass panel to greatly improve visibility. The former car's MacPherson struts and torsion bars were replaced by a more sophisticated wishbone arrangement. The line-up of CRX powerplants also were upgraded. The fuel-frugal CRX HF was powered by a 1.5 liter four rated at 62 hp and 56 mpg on the federal highway cycle. The midline CRX had 16 valves for 1988 and churned up 92 hp—one more horsepower than 1987's Si model. That's because the 1988 Si used a larger 1.6 liter engine and 16 valves to generate 105 hp and 0-60 mph times of 8.2 seconds.

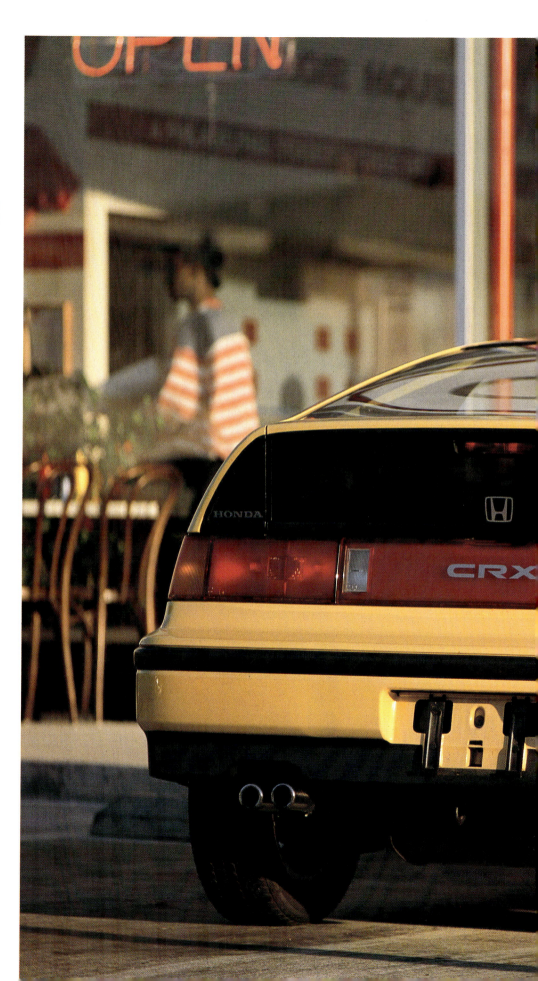

The automotive success story of 1986 has to be Acura Automobile Division, the newly formed premium line of Honda Motor Company. Acura's entry in the luxury performance segment of the US market has Mercedes-Benz, Volvo and BMW running scared and Toyota and Nissan running to catch up. The upscale models Acura offers are the Legend Sedan, Legend Coupe and Integra three-door and five-door sports sedans. The Acura automobiles have been winners on the sales floor, in award competitions, in consumer satisfaction and at the racetrack. In sales, Acura sold 52,869 units for the 1986 calendar year. The following year, Acura's first full sales year, sales reached 109,470—outdistancing Volvo, 106,539; Mercedes-Benz, 90,832; and BMW, 89,487. The strong sales have been boosted by numerous awards Acura cars have received including 10 Best Cars, Car and Driver magazine, for the Integra and Legend Coupe; 10 Best Cars Based on Value, Road & Track magazine, for the Legend Sedan and Coupe; and 1987 Import Car of the Year, Motor Trend magazine, for the Legend coupe. Acura also took top honors in the J. D. Power Consumer Satisfaction survey in 1987 and 1988; Mercedes-Benz was second. On the racing circuit, the Integra has dominated the IMSA International Sedan series, winning titles in 1986, 1987 and 1988 with the Comptech racing team of Doug Peterson and Parker Johnstone.

Since it hit the international auto show circuit in 1979, the Isuzu Impulse has been on a fast track. Originally a concept car and styling exercise by famed Italian designer Giorgio Giugiaro, the Ace of Clubs was pushed into production when it was widely acclaimed by the auto industry and motoring public. Introduced in Japan in 1981 as the Impulse, the car was a faithful recreation of Giugiaro's exotic shape. The same steeply raked windshield, clamshell body panels and flush window glass carried over to the production car. The Impulse, which reached the US market in 1983, received a turbocharger and intercooler in 1985. With 140 hp from two liters on tap, the zoomy Impulse Turbo now had the power to match its looks. The Impulse's suspension and handling got a make-over for 1988. The engineers at Lotus tried numerous spring, shock absorber and tire combinations on the four-place sports coupe. The testing and development resulted in greatly improved roadability and a "Handling by Lotus" badge.

The concept-car heritage of the Isuzu Impulse can be seen in the sophisticated and very functional instrument panel, dashboard layout and interior design. As with the body design, the dash concept was faithfully carried over from the show car to the production model. The Impulse was the first production car to make use of a pair of pods mounted at fingertip length away from the steering wheel. Without taking a hand off the steering wheel or eyes off the road, the Impulse driver can activate the light, turn signals, windshield wipers and climate control. The center console houses a multi-function monitor with a display that can tell the time, elapsed time, instantaneous mileage computation, fuel remaining, date, and distance traveled. An adjustable steering column with a memory feature, power windows and air conditioning are standard. The Turbo version has a driver seat with seven-way adjustment for side bolsters, lumbar support and thigh support. Another unique interior feature is rear seats that have reclining seatbacks. The seats also can be folded down for increased cargo capacity. Impulse enthusiasts rally around the Impulse International Auto Club based in California. The club's magazine is called the Pulse.

Technically more exotic than a Ferrari V-12 engine is the fuel-injected, intercooled, turbocharged rotary engine found only in the Mazda RX-7 Turbo. Mazda has raised the Wankel engine to its highest level ever; a level that revs up to 182 hp at 6500 rpm and a 0-60 mph time of 6.7 seconds. The Turbo model, recognized instantly by its aggressive hood scoop, shows off its muscle with a deep front air dam, side skirts and a rear spoiler. The aerodynamic aids allow the Turbo to slip through the airstream with a drag coefficient of just 0.31. The Turbo performance package is rounded off with 16 inch alloy wheels, sports-tuned suspension, five-speed manual gearbox, limited-slip differential and four-wheel ventilated disc brakes. On the creature-comfort side, the Turbo has virtually every luxury feature standard including electric sunroof, air conditioning, tilt steering wheel, 100 watt sound system, power windows, door locks and side mirrors.

The zenith of the Mazda RX-7 sports car has been reached ten years after its introduction. The complete RX-7 fleet now includes five distinctive models—base SE, aerodynamically styled GTU, luxury GXL, high-powered Turbo and convertible. While the convertible is not available with the 182 hp engine used in the Turbo, it generates more than enough excitement with its topless motoring. The convertible, powered by the normally-aspirated 146 hp engine, has brought the roadster into the modern era. The convertible roof is power-controlled and folds completely down at the touch of a button. The top itself has three stages—open, half-open as in a Porsche Targa, and closed. Mazda engineers also have made the convertible a car that can be driven top-down year around. That's made possible by a special high-output heater, exclusive on the convertible, and an ingenious device called the Windblocker. The Windblocker is a flat panel located behind the seatbacks. When flipped up, it creates a dam that dramatically reduces turbulence and wind chill in the interior.

The Mitsubishi Starion ESI-R is a "turnkey" car for sports car enthusiasts. There's nothing more to add or modify, it's all there from the factory. Mitsubishi did the aftermarket a great disservice by equipping the Starion with all the good stuff. Take for example the suspension. There's no need to upgrade when the Starion has eight-way adjustable shocks, four-wheel disc brakes, antilock rear brakes and eight-inch front and nine-inch rear wheels. The 16 inch tire setup is even trick, with larger 225/45VR50 rear tires complementing the 225/VR50 front tires. In the engine compartment, Mitsubishi again has done the modifications. The 2.6 liter, four-cylinder engine is fuel injected, intercooled and turbocharged to the tune of 188 hp at 5000 rpm. Twin balance shafts spinning at twice the crankshaft speed ensure the big four is smooth and free of vibrations. Transmission choices are a five-speed gearbox or a four-speed automatic. The turnkey Starion really works—Dave Wolin's Mitsubishi team won the Sports Car Club of America Showroom Stock Endurance championship for Class A in 1987. The Class A competition included Nissan 300ZX, Toyota Supra, Audi Quattro and Mazda RX-7.

Pretty in white is the 1988 Special Edition Nissan 300ZX. The basic body style, which was brand-new in 1984, has been freshened up with a face-lift from the Nissan Design International, Inc., styling group in San Diego, California. The cosmetic surgery included smoothing and integrating the hood, bumper and air dam into a unified, flowing shape. The cleaner look also reduced the ZX's frontal area and improved the aerodynamic drag coefficient. The new-look ZX body sits on either a 91.3 inch or 99.2 inch wheelbase platform. The longer version is for the 2+2 model that has a pair of occasional seats. The powerplant used throughout the three-model line-up is a three-liter V-6. In normally-aspirated form, the V-6 engine is rated at 165 hp at 5200 rpm. When under pressure from a turbocharger, the horsepower level jumps to 205. A smaller turbo unit and an increase in compression ratio to 8.3:1 gives the Turbo improved low-end and mid-range response. The top-of-the-line Turbo also has a limited-slip differential, three-way cockpit-adjustable shock absorbers and 16 inch alloy wheels and Goodyear Eagle VR50 radials. ZX owners can have their choice of either traditional analog instruments or an optional digital instrument panel.

There is more to the Special Edition Nissan 300ZX Turbo than meets the eye. Beneath the all-white pearl exterior with white, 16 inch wheels and European-style front air dam, are the best seats in the business, multi-adjustable Recaro cloth seats. The German-made seats are the perfect match to the well-turned-out and thought-out interior. From the cockpit and even while the car is in motion, the driver can select from firm, normal or soft settings on the three-way adjustable shock absorbers. The long list of luxury interior features includes leather-wrapped, three-spoke steering wheel, power windows, cruise control, power steering, power door locks, theft deterrent system, air conditioning and a tilt steering wheel. An available audio package consists of an 80 watt stereo system with eight speakers and a graphic equalizer. An optional electronic equipment package includes a power driver's seat, premium stereo system, automatic temperature control, power outside mirrors with a defogging function, and audio and speed controls that are incorporated in the steering wheel. The standard analog gauges also can be replaced with a full digital instrument panel.

Nissan's California design center gave the Pulsar NX multiple personalities. Like the popular Japanese Transformer toy robots, the Pulsar can change itself to meet the driver's needs. Need a sporty convertible? Then lift off the panels from the Pulsar's T-bar roof and remove the rear hatch. Remove just the rear hatch and you have a quasi-pickup. With the optional SportBak installed in place of the hatch lid, the versatile Pulsar becomes a sporty station wagon. The very different vehicles the Pulsar can become all share the same 95.7 inch wheelbase and 166.5 inch platform. The available engines also can determine if the Pulsar is a fuel-efficient economy car or a pocket rocket. The standard four-cylinder engine displaces 1.6 liters and produces 69 hp at 5000 rpm. The more spirited choice is the 1.8 liter, 16 valve powerplant that kicks out 125 hp. The pair of engines can be mated to either a five-speed manual gearbox or a three-speed automatic.

The easily installed SportBak option transforms the sporty Nissan Pulsar NX into a functional mini sports wagon. The Pulsar's rear seat folds down to further increase cargo capacity. When replacing the previous Pulsar that was introduced in 1983, Nissan designers sought an all-new modular design that would allow the new car to appeal to a large and diverse group of drivers in the small specialty-car market. The front-wheel-drive Pulsar does this by offering an economy car, a sports car and a practical car all in the same package. According to Nissan, the demographics of Pulsar buyers range from single men and women starting careers, to young couples with small children, to middle-aged buyers who need a second car to commute to work. The XE model has power rack-and-pinion steering and single-point fuel injection. The high-performance, 16 valve engine has multi-port fuel injection and is found on the SE variation. In addition to the potent engine, the SE adds a front air dam, woven cloth interior seats, 14 inch alloy wheels with 195/60 radials and a rear antiroll bar.

Once the top-of-the-line Celica, the Toyota Supra became its own distinctive model in 1982. By splitting off the two cars, Toyota now had the Celica in the sports coupe market and the upscale Supra in the luxury performance division. The all-new Supra had a 102.8 inch wheelbase, up nearly four inches from the Celica. While marketed separately from the Celica, the Supra and Celica shared many common body components from the windshield on back. The Supra also had an inline six-cylinder engine displacing 2.8 liters and producing 165 hp. The Supra powerplant featured double overhead camshafts, but only two valves per cylinder. The powerplant, which later would become the foundation for more exotic and powerful versions, was mated to either a five-speed manual gearbox or a four-speed electrically controlled overdrive automatic transmission with a high-performance torque converter. In place of the Celica's solid rear axle, Toyota upgraded the Supra rear suspension to a semi-trailing arm independent system. The Supra also had an upgraded interior with multi-adjustable seats, premium upholstery material, tilt steering wheel and a comprehensive instrument panel with tachometer, speedometer, oil pressure, coolant temperature, voltmeter and fuel level.

The MR2 Supercharged is quite an encore to Toyota's mid-engine sportster. The standard MR2 is powered by a spirited 16 valve, 1.6 liter engine pumping out 115 hp at 6600 rpm. Transmission choices include a five-speed gearbox or a four-speed automatic. The mid-mounted engine in the 91.3 inch wheelbase sportster made for quick and responsive handling that rivaled race cars. The four-wheel disc brakes are first class and offer superior braking performance with 60 percent of the weight carried over the rear wheels. The 7500 rpm redline makes for peppy acceleration, but the sophisticated, four-wheel independent chassis is more capable than the standard normally aspirated engine. Toyota evened up the balance of power by installing a Rootes-type supercharger that hiked horsepower 30 percent to 145. As the horsepower figure climbed, the 0-60 mph times dropped nearly two seconds to seven seconds flat. The MR2 Supercharged has a top speed in excess of 130 mph. The MR2 Supercharged package also includes a deep front spoiler, rear deck wing and aero side skirts. Wider alloy wheels and a T-bar roof are also included, as shown on the chapter's opening pages.

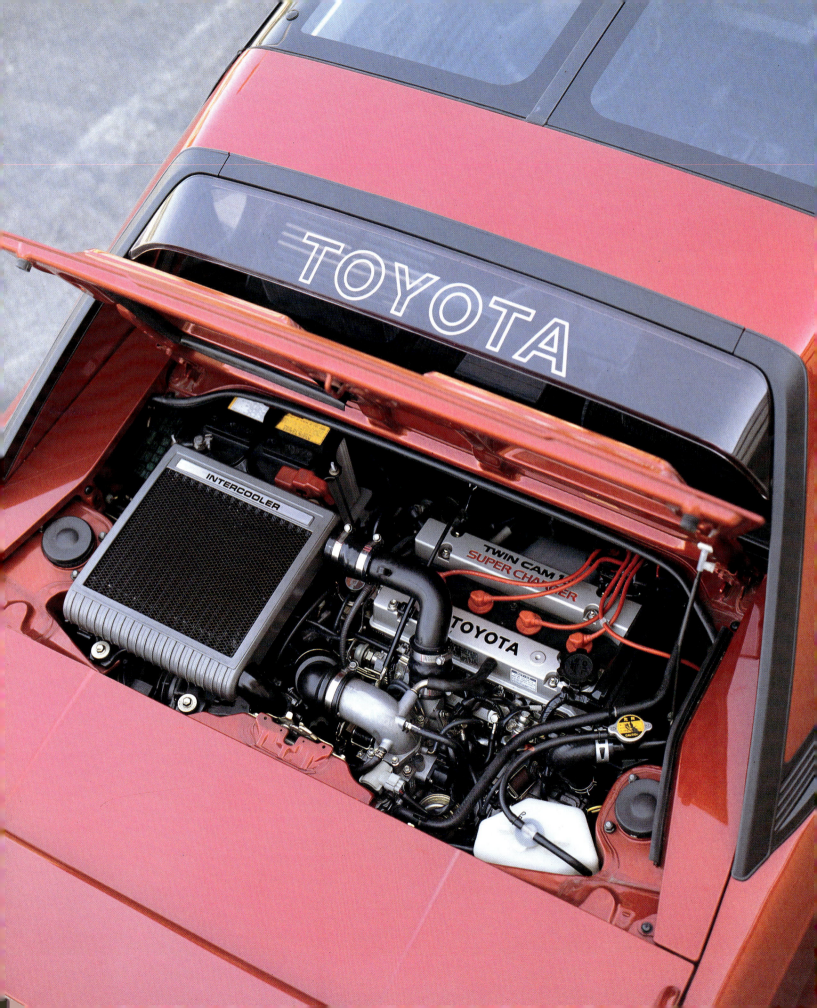

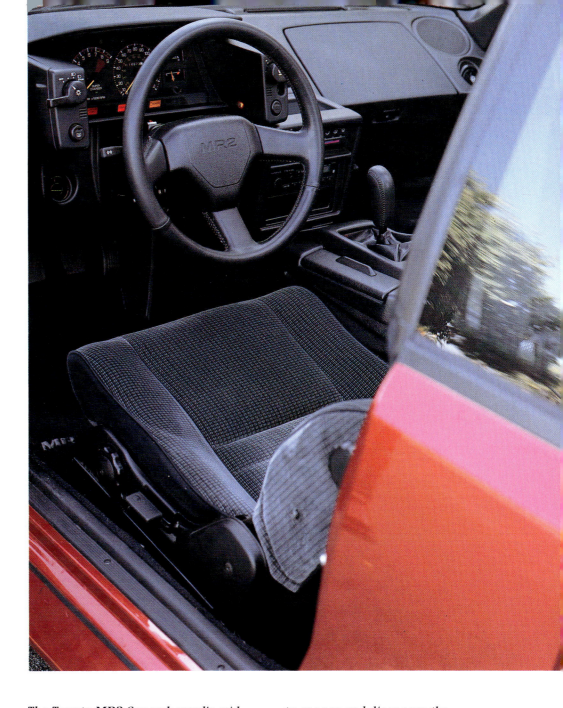

The Toyota MR2 Supercharged's mid-engine layout makes for a cozy interior. The driver has full instrumentation to monitor the state-of-the-art, 16 valve powerplant with Rootes-type supercharger. The supercharger works in conjunction with an air-to-air intercooler that lowers the temperature of the compressed intake charge to provide a denser fuel mix and more horsepower. The ingenious system uses an electronic clutch on the supercharger to engage and disengage the supercharger compressor. When extra power is not needed the clutch unit freewheels and no power or fuel is wasted turning the compressor. When accelerated briskly, the system engages the compressor and begins boosting performance. This on-demand system gives the MR2 Supercharged the best of both worlds—good fuel economy and excellent performance.

The 1988 Toyota Celica All-Trac Turbo is an all-star in the automotive world. Inspired by the latest Pro Rally racers, the heart of the 3,197 pound All-Trac is its full-time, four-wheel-drive system. The viscous center coupling makes for great traction and handling on all surfaces. Antilock brakes are optional on the 99.4 inch wheelbase All-Trac. The power for all four wheels is generated by a two-liter, 16 valve four-cylinder engine that has been turbocharged to produce 40 percent more horsepower than the standard unit. Helping to pump the horsepower up to 190 at 6000 rpm is a liquid-cooled intercooler. Traditional intercoolers are air-to-air, but the All-Trac intercooler uses engine coolant to reduce the temperature of the compressed intake air even further. The result is a denser combustion charge and exceptional power output. Flared fenders are needed for clearance for the 14 inch alloy wheels and 205/60 radial tires. All-Trac drivers can shift for themselves with a five-speed manual gearbox, or let the optional four-speed automatic make the choices. A front air dam with integrated foglights and a rear spoiler round out the All-Trac package.

America's love affair with the convertible forced Toyota to meet that demand with a topless Celica. As with the original 1984 Celica convertible, the 1988 edition starts out life as a coupe in Japan. The car is then shipped to the United States to the Automotive Specialty Company (ASC) in Rancho Dominguez, California. There ASC chops the top of the 99.4 inch wheelbase Celica, adds reinforcements to the chassis and installs the power top, rear quarter windows and a one-piece fold-down seat. The Celica convertible is based on the GT model coupe and is powered by a two-liter, four-cylinder engine. The double overhead cam powerplant is rated at 115 hp. But Americans are not the only lovers of open-air motoring, as Toyota Motor Sales, U.S.A., exports 100 US-modified Celica convertibles to Japan each month. Since a Japan-bound automobile must be right-hand drive, the Japanese-market Celica convertibles must make two trips across the Pacific Ocean. Partially built, right-hand-drive Celicas are shipped from Japan to ASC, where they are converted and sent back to Japan. The Celica convertible is in high demand in Japan because of the exclusivity of the value added by the US modifications.

Into the future

A moving target is hard to hit, and the Japanese are not standing still. They are continuing to advance their world automotive leadership by pushing the development of new auto designs and concepts to the limit.

An example of that commitment is Nissan Design International, Inc., headquartered not in Japan, but at San Diego, California.

"The idea of building a design studio somewhere overseas originated about five years ago," said Nissan Executive Vice President H. Takahashi at the California studio's opening ceremonies in 1983, "when we began to feel a need to bring a more international flair into the automotive design area in order to strengthen our overall product development capabilities."

Takahashi said the United States was chosen, over the twenty countries on six continents on which Nissan has plants, because of its responsiveness to the international automotive market.

"We chose the US on the grounds that it is the most advanced country on the globe in the design field, consistently spearheading the establishment of new international trends," said Takahashi.

Nissan states San Diego was chosen because it had "a stimulating atmosphere, progressive spirit and an energetic lifestyle conducive to stimulating creativity. It was close enough to the car culture of Los Angeles to monitor new trends, yet far enough away to be unduly influenced by them. Also, since San Diego has no connection with the auto industry, it was a place where Nissan's designers could start with a clean slate."

Nissan's location choice has proven correct. Automobiles designed at the San Diego facility have won numerous international design awards and have proven to be strong sellers worldwide.

The San Diego studio was directly responsible for the 1986½ Hardbody light-truck series, the 1987 Pathfinder sports utility vehicle, the innovative 1987 Pulsar NX and the facelift of the 1987 300ZX sports car.

These vehicles have won many prestigious awards throughout the world. The Pulsar NX was named Car of the Year for 1987 in Japan, Canada and Australia, as well as winning the IDEA and Grand Mark from Japan's Ministry of International Trade and Industry. The four-wheel-drive Pathfinder has been 4x4 of the Year in Australia, Canada and America, and was given a superior design award by the *Japan Economic News*.

The man behind the award-winning designs and Nissan Design International is Gerald P. Hirshberg, the former chief designer at both Pontiac and Buick. Some of his notable creations include the GTO and Firebird for Pontiac and the Buick Electra and LeSabre.

Hirshberg said he ended his sixteen-year career at General Motors because of Nissan's commitment to the design center.

"The fact that Nissan was not just creating another vague 'advanced' concept center, but instead was committing to a real production design facility," said Hirshberg about his reasons for leaving General Motors. "The fact that there was the opportunity to freely share in the shaping and developing of the methodology, structure and facility was also highly appealing. Finally, the chance for deep intercultural involvement with engineers and other disciplines. It seemed that Nissan was about to carry internationalism to higher and more profound levels."

Nissan Design International, located east of the University of California at San Diego, has a college campus atmosphere. The 43,000 square foot facility is situated on 6.5 acres and includes large studios and workshops, a well-stocked library, a landscaped central courtyard and a tennis court.

The design center, combining the best of both Eastern and Western resources, is set up as an autonomous corporation that operates independently. The center has a high degree of freedom and privacy not possible within a typical large automotive "redtape" corporation.

The $4.7 million facility has a staff of nearly thirty designers, industrial sculptors and engineers. The diverse staff allows the design center to engineer every aspect of a vehicle, with the goal of actual production.

Hirshberg said the marriage of Japanese cars designed in America is a good one. Historically, he said, the Japanese honor tradition to the extreme of not wanting to develop new ideas and concepts. Meanwhile, Americans are makers of tradition.

Together the Japanese heritage and new American ideas form an intercultural energy that makes possible creative cars like the Pulsar NX and Pathfinder.

In addition to its automotive work, Nissan Design International has designed such diversified products as medical instruments, audio equipment, motels, and outboard engines for Nissan's marine division. Graphic design programs also have been contracted with businesses and universities.

However, its primary task is to look at the world with a fresh eye and develop vehicles that will make Nissan and Japan a leader in automotive design.

The Nissan Design International, Inc. has a bright future because it has a bold past. That history includes the revolutionary Nissan Pulsar NX, the first true modular production car. Looking back at the Pulsar's beginnings is Doug Wilson, a staff designer at the drawings. As Wilson's design evolved wagon. The evolution of Wilson's initial design resulted in the Pulsar going into production and winning the prestigious Japan Car of the Year award. The Pulsar also met with critical approval in Europe. With the Pulsar NX, the Nissan Design International staff proved that a design that was focused mainly at American and other Western markets could have universal appeal and acclaim. On the previous spread this chapter opens with a design exercise from Mazda's Irvine, California, facility. It is but one of a number of futuristic concepts to entertain us.

At Nissan Design International, staffers doodle and get paid for it. The first step in the series of many for an automobile design to reach production is doodling some ideas and then advancing the best elements of the doodles into more detailed drawings. Following three-dimensional-style "image sketches," the design is transformed by industrial sculptors into a scale model in clay. The clay forms allow a real-world look at the design from top to bottom and from side to side. Lines, shadows and impressions not seen on paper are readily revealed in the clay work. The clay form also can be scrutinized by a wind tunnel to examine, determine and improve its aerodynamic fingerprint. Flaws in the aerodynamics of the design can be uncovered and corrected in the scale model stage for much less expense in time and money than in larger and actual size models.

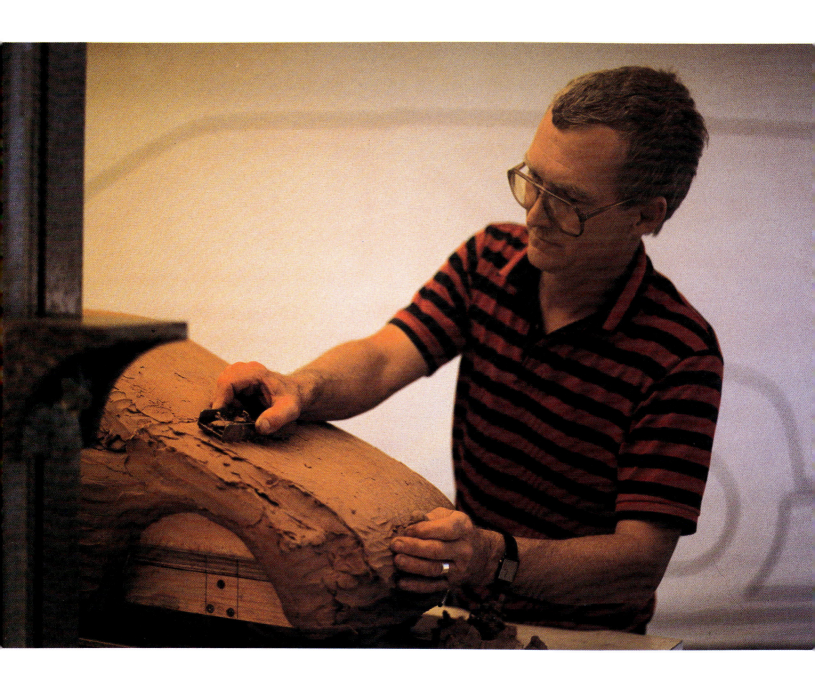

Gerald P. Hirshberg works with an industrial sculptor on a full-size scale model of clay. To reach this stage, a concept of a new automobile requires the collaboration with all the different disciplines involved in making a car— production, chassis body design, aerodynamics, engineering, interior design and much more. For example, a ski-slope front-end design looks fine on paper and in clay, but do the engineering and chassis divisions have an engine and powertrain that will fit underneath? The interior must be functional for driver and passenger. The clay design must be able to be translated in the metal, plastic and glass of a production car. A more recent concern is for safety, the crashworthiness of the design and the energy absorption of the interior. Among the numerous cosmetic decisions is the design of the wheels. Note the dozens of wheel styles posted on the back wall being considered for the vehicle. On the following pages is a model of one of the proposed 300 ZX replacements photographed for the first time. It came from the pen of Doug Wilson at the San Diego studio. It wasn't the one accepted.

Nissan Design International chief designer Gerald P. Hirshberg looks over a scale model of a radical, futuristic car created by the San Diego studio. The natural light of the studio's tree-filled courtyard best shows off the vehicle's fully enclosed wheels, blunt nose, large greenhouse and jellybean shape. The scale model concept car best illustrates why Hirshberg left General Motors Corporation. While GM and other auto makers have small advance design studios similar to the San Diego facility, Hirshberg believes they are set up to do projects that may never see the light of day. The goal of Nissan Design International, however, is to design vehicles that will actually be produced. Hirshberg's studio is the first and only such concept house capable of doing production-ready designs. It is staffed with teams of American and Japanese engineers who have the experience and production knowledge. With that commitment, any project developed by the Nissan studio is more than just a concept, it has a viable future as a production car. Suddenly the jellybean design posed with Hirshberg does not look so radical or futuristic. With Nissan Design International, it could be reality in the very near future.